A Midsummer Night's Dream

by
William Shakespeare

CORE CLASSICS®

ISBN 978-1-933486-91-8
COPYRIGHT © 2019 CORE KNOWLEDGE FOUNDATION
ALL RIGHTS RESERVED
PRINTED IN CANADA

CORE KNOWLEDGE FOUNDATION
801 EAST HIGH STREET
CHARLOTTESVILLE, VIRGINIA 22902

www.coreknowledge.org

Table of Contents

Introduction by E.D. Hirsch, Jr.
I

Shakespeare and the Globe
VII

A Midsummer Night's Dream
A Story Based on the Play by William Shakespeare
1

A Midsummer Night's Dream
An Abridged Version of the Play by William Shakespeare

Introduction to the Play
28

A Note on Poetry and Prose
30

Cast of Characters
32

Act 1
34

Act 2
68

Act 3
102

Act 4
148

Act 5
162

INTRODUCTION

"He was not of an age but for all time!" A poet, Ben Jonson, wrote these words about a fellow poet who had recently died. What do the words mean? They mean that the poet will be remembered forever. They mean that he wrote of matters that will be meaningful and beautifully expressed for all people, in every time and place in the future.

Who is this timeless writer? He is William Shakespeare, the greatest poet and playwright who ever lived. He wrote his plays in England four centuries ago–that's four hundred years–and yet today in the United States, more theaters put on plays by Shakespeare than by any other playwright.

Although Shakespeare wrote in English–some of the most beautiful and powerful English words you will ever hear or speak–his plays are loved around the world, even in translation. The stories that Shakespeare tells, the characters he created, and his magnificent way with words capture the imaginations of people whose language is not English. His plays have been translated into many other languages—Spanish, Japanese, Russian, and many more. Even in those other languages his way with words shines through.

Shakespeare wrote at least thirty-seven plays. He sometimes acted in them himself. In his lifetime, Shakespeare's plays were enjoyed by people from all walks of life—by butchers and blacksmiths and shopkeepers, as well as by scholars and dukes and even Queen Elizabeth herself.

Keep in mind that Shakespeare wrote plays in handwriting, not in printed books. Indeed, if it weren't for the efforts of his friends and fellow actors, who collected the handwritten scripts of Shakespeare's plays after his death, we might not have them now.

Shakespeare didn't picture people sitting around and reading his plays in a book. He wrote them to be seen and heard. They come to life when you see and hear them (or perform them), or when they are acted out in a theater, or on a movie screen, or in a school classroom or auditorium.

This book will introduce you to one of

INTRODUCTION

Shakespeare's best-loved and funniest comedies, *A Midsummer Night's Dream*. You may find that some of Shakespeare's language seems strange at first. This is not surprising: after all, the English language has changed a lot over the past four hundred years. This book provides notes to help you understand some words that may be unfamiliar or no longer in use. But it doesn't take long to get comfortable hearing or speaking Shakespeare's words. When the actor on the stage asks, "What hast thou done?" it is clear that he means, "What have you done?" On the stage, when spoken and acted, the language may sometimes sound old-fashioned, but its power and poetry will pull you into the story coming to life before your eyes.

There is a long tradition of introducing young people to Shakespeare by retelling his plays as stories. In the early 1800s, Charles and Mary Lamb wrote a popular book called *Tales from Shakespeare*, which told many of the best-loved plays as stories for children. In this tradition, the book you are now reading begins by presenting *A Midsummer Night's Dream* in the form of a short story.

We then follow the story with a script of the play, a shortened version that can be performed in about an hour. *A Midsummer Night's Dream* will come to life when you gather with classmates, friends, or family members to read the script aloud, or, even better, to act it out. It doesn't have to be fancy. You don't need gorgeous costumes or high-tech special effects. Just heed the advice of Hamlet, one of Shakespeare's greatest characters, who says that you only need to "speak the speech" naturally, letting the words help you express the emotions. Whether you are watching *A Midsummer Night's Dream* or performing in it, it will be fun!

E. D. Hirsch Jr.
Charlottesville, Virginia

V

A COLLECTION OF SHAKESPEARE'S PLAYS, KNOWN AS THE FIRST FOLIO, WAS PUBLISHED IN 1623.

VII

SHAKESPEARE AND THE GLOBE

In 1564 William Shakespeare was born in England, in the town of Stratford-upon-Avon, about ninety miles northwest of the great bustling city of London. Shakespeare is sometimes called the "Bard of Avon." (*Bard* is another word for poet.)

In Shakespeare's time, well-off boys attended school. Girls stayed home. Young Will probably spent long hours learning Latin, Greek, the Bible, and English history. It seems Will didn't enjoy school much: in one of his plays, he described "the whining schoolboy, with his satchel . . . creeping like [a] snail unwillingly to school."

There's a lot about Shakespeare's life we don't know. Over the years scholars have examined the available evidence—there's not much of it—and have tried to put together a picture of the playwright's life. We do know that eighteen-year-old William married twenty-six-year-old Anne Hathaway in 1582. Over the next few years, Anne gave birth to their daughter Susanna, followed by twins, a daughter named Judith, and a son named Hamnet.

Shakespeare did not linger very long in Stratford-upon-Avon. By 1592, Shakespeare was in London and establishing a reputation as a playwright, actor, and poet.

When Shakespeare wrote his plays, England was ruled by Queen Elizabeth I and later by King James I. Elizabeth was a powerful and intelligent leader, and very popular with the English people. The arts thrived during the reign of Queen Elizabeth. She filled her court with poets, playwrights, and musicians.

Many of Shakespeare's plays were performed in the Globe Theatre, which was built in 1599 on the south bank of the Thames River in London. The Globe was a wooden, circular building with an open courtyard in the middle. The theater could hold up to 2,500 people.

At the Globe, people who didn't have much money could pay a penny to stand in the courtyard and watch the play; they were called the groundlings. Richer people could buy seats in the galleries, which were along three sides of the theater and were covered by a roof to protect the audience from the sun or a sudden rain. Performances were given only in daylight and only in good weather.

Queen Elizabeth I

In Shakespeare's time, only men acted on stage. No women were allowed to be actors! The women's parts were played by young boys who still had high voices and no beards.

In 1613, a cannon fired as part of a performance of Shakespeare's play titled *Henry VIII* set fire to the Globe's thatched roof, and the theater burned to the ground. In the 1990s the theater was rebuilt very near its original location. So, if you visit London today, you can still see a Shakespeare play at the new Globe Theatre.

THE GLOBE THEATRE, AS IT APPEARED IN SHAKESPEARE'S DAY

XI

TITANIA, THE FAIRY QUEEN

A MIDSUMMER NIGHT'S DREAM

A STORY

BASED ON THE PLAY BY

WILLIAM SHAKESPEARE

1

Long ago in the city of Athens, there was a cruel law that gave a father the power to choose his daughter's husband—and if the daughter refused, she could be put to death. This law was so cruel that no one could remember it ever being enforced. But one day, a cranky old man named Egeus came running to the court of the leader of Athens, Duke Theseus.

Egeus dragged behind him his daughter, Hermia. And closely behind followed two young men, Lysander and Demetrius. Both wanted to marry Hermia. Hermia, however, wanted to marry

Lysander. But her father demanded that she marry Demetrius.

Bowing to Duke Theseus, old Egeus cried out, "Full of **vexation** come I, with complaint against my child, my daughter Hermia. I have chosen Demetrius to be Hermia's husband. But Lysander has stolen her affection. If she will not obey me and marry Demetrius, then I claim the law of Athens against my daughter! She must go to Demetrius in marriage, or to her death!"

vexation: the state of being worried and annoyed

As Duke Theseus heard these angry claims, he pressed the hand of the tall woman standing by his side, the warrior queen Hippolyta. Theseus and Hippolyta were preparing to be married in a few days. The duke wished that Egeus would just go away, but he knew that he had to deal with the matter. And he also knew that he could not ignore the old law.

"What say you, Hermia?" asked Theseus. "Demetrius is a worthy gentleman."

"So is Lysander," replied Hermia.

Lysander cried out, "I am beloved of

beauteous Hermia. But Demetrius **pledged** his love to our friend, Helena. And she still **dotes upon** him."

> **pledged:** promised
>
> **dotes upon:** adores; shows excessive affection and attention

"Your grace," said Hermia to the duke, "what is the worst that will happen to me if I refuse to wed Demetrius?"

The duke sighed. "The law is the law, and I cannot change it," he said. "You must either marry Demetrius or be put to death. Or," the duke added, seeking some less terrible **option**, "you must live alone and apart, as a nun."

> **option:** choice

A short while later, when Hermia was alone with Lysander, she buried her head on his shoulder and cried, "**Alas**, I must choose love by another's eyes!"

> **alas:** an expression of sadness

Lysander stroked her hair and said, "The course of true love never did run smooth." Then he smiled—he had thought of a plan! "Hear me, Hermia," he said. "I have an aunt who lives miles away from Athens. If we go there, then the cruel law cannot reach us. Tomorrow night, sneak away from your father's house and meet me in the wood just outside the city." From there, he explained, they would make their way to his aunt's house and then get married.

"My good Lysander!" cried Hermia, wrapping her arms around him. "Tomorrow truly will I meet you in the wood, where I have sometimes walked among the flowers with my dear friend Helena."

Just then, who should appear but Helena? She saw her friends with their arms around each other, and she sighed. Oh, she thought, if only Demetrius loved me as Lysander loves Hermia!

"Fair Helena!" cried Hermia and ran to her friend. Hermia quickly told Helena about Lysander's plan to sneak away from Athens and get married. "And in the wood," said Hermia, "where you and I have rested on sweet **primrose beds**, Lysander and I will meet tomorrow night. **Farewell**, sweet playfellow. Pray thou for us. And good luck **grant thee** thy Demetrius!"

primrose beds: beds of pale, yellow flowers
farewell: goodbye
grant thee: give you

As Helena waved farewell to her friends, who were walking away hand in hand, she began to think. Her thoughts took a foolish and jealous turn. "Throughout Athens," she said to herself, "I am thought as fair as Hermia. But what of that? Demetrius thinks not so. He dotes on Hermia. Though once, before he looked on her, he swore that he was only mine. I will go tell him of fair Hermia's **flight**!"

> **flight:** running away

And so Helena rushed to tell Demetrius about Hermia and Lysander's secret plan to sneak away to get married. For this, she thought, Demetrius might love me again! And just as the **fickle** Demetrius was likely to go to the wood in search of Hermia, Helena was more than likely to follow him.

> **fickle:** changeable in affection or interests

2

Elsewhere in Athens, a group of workmen gathered at the home of Peter Quince, a carpenter. They were planning to put on a play as part of the festivities to celebrate the wedding of Theseus to Hippolyta in a few days.

"Now," said Peter Quince to his fellow

workmen, "our play is called *The Most **Lamentable** Comedy and Most Cruel Death of **Pyramus and Thisbe**.*" Quince, who had taken on the duties of a director, then proceeded to name the parts each man would play.

lamentable: sorrowful

Pyramus and Thisbe: the main characters in a tragic love story from ancient mythology

To a weaver named Nick Bottom—who loved to act though he had little talent for it—Quince assigned the part of the romantic hero, Pyramus. To young Francis Flute, Quince gave the role of Thisbe.

"What is Thisbe?" asked Flute. "A wandering knight?"

"No," said Quince. "Thisbe is the lady that Pyramus must love."

"Nay!" cried Flute, as the other workmen laughed and hooted. "Let me not play a woman! I have a beard coming."

Bottom leaped up and cried, "Let me play Thisbe too!"

"No," replied Quince. "You must play Pyramus. And Flute, you Thisbe."

As Bottom sat down with a disappointed sigh, Quince assigned the remaining parts. But when

Quince gave the part of the lion to a carpenter named Snug, Bottom could not **restrain** himself. In great excitement he jumped up and cried, "Let me play the lion too! I will roar, that I will make the duke say, 'Let him roar again. Let him roar again!'"

> **restrain:** keep under control

"You can play no part but Pyramus!" snapped Quince.

Bottom turned away in a huff and stared at the wall. Quince could see that he would need to **coax** Bottom back into the play. "Of course you know," said Quince to Bottom, "that Pyramus is a sweet-faced man, a most lovely gentleman-like man. Therefore you must play Pyramus."

> **coax:** to persuade through flattery

"Well," said Bottom, pretending some hesitation—although in fact he was bursting with eagerness to begin— "I will undertake it!"

"Tomorrow night," said Quince, "we will rehearse by moonlight. Let us meet in the wood, a mile without the town"–the very same wood, though the workmen did not know it, where Hermia and Lysander had agreed to meet.

3

This wood was also the favorite **haunt** of the magical beings known as fairies. Oberon, the king of the fairies, and Titania, the queen, with all their followers, held their midnight **revels** in this wood. When the moon shone, they often danced to merry music among the flowers.

haunt: a place where people often go

revels: lively entertainments

But lately there had been neither music nor dancing, because of a **quarrel** between Oberon and Titania. The cause of this unhappy disagreement was that Titania refused to give Oberon a certain little boy. The mother of this boy, who had been Titania's friend, had fallen sick and died. Upon her death, the fairy queen took the child to raise him in the wood. But Oberon wanted the child for his own.

quarrel: argument

It was now the night on which Lysander and Hermia were to meet in the wood. Titania was out walking with her fairy maids, and they chanced to meet Oberon, attended by his fairy followers.

"**Ill met** by moonlight, proud Titania," growled the fairy king.

"What, jealous Oberon!" snapped the fairy queen in reply.

"Why should Titania **cross** her Oberon?" asked the fairy king. "Give me the boy to be my **page**."

> **ill met:** unhappily or unfortunately encountered
>
> **cross:** oppose, resist, defy
>
> **page:** a young boy who attends upon and assists a person such as a king

"Set your heart at rest," answered the queen. "Your whole fairy kingdom buys not the boy from me." And then she left in great anger.

"Well! Go your way," said Oberon. "Before the morning dawns I will **torment** you for this **injury**."

Oberon then called the **mischievous** fairy named Robin Goodfellow, better known as Puck, who was Oberon's favorite.

> **torment:** to cause pain or distress
>
> **injury:** hurtful act
>
> **mischievous:** naughty, fond of playing pranks and tricks

"Come **hither**, Puck," said Oberon to this merry little wanderer of the night. "Fetch me the flower that maidens call 'Love in Idleness.' If the juice of that flower be laid on the eyelids of those who sleep, it will make them, when they awake, fall in love with the first thing they

> **hither:** here, to this place

see. Some of the juice of that flower I will drop on the eyelids of my Titania when she is asleep. When she awakes, she will fall madly in love with the first thing she sees, though it be a lion, a bear, a wolf, or a monkey. Before I take this charm off her

PUCK LOVED MISCHIEF AND PRANKS.

sight, I will make her give me that boy."

Puck, who loved mischief and **pranks**, was highly pleased with this scheme and sped away to fetch the magic flower.

pranks: practical jokes

While Oberon was waiting for Puck to return, he saw Demetrius and Helena enter the wood. He overheard Demetrius speak unkind words to Helena, who had eagerly followed him.

"I love thee not, therefore pursue me not!" Demetrius snapped at Helena. "In plainest truth I tell you, I do not and cannot love you."

"And even for that do I love you the more!" cried Helena.

Demetrius looked around. "Where is fair Hermia?" he said. Then he turned and ran away.

"I'll follow thee!" cried Helena and ran after him as swiftly as she could.

The fairy king had watched all this with interest. "Before this night is over," whispered Oberon as Helena ran off, "he shall seek thy love!"

At this moment, Puck returned with the little

purple flower. "Welcome, wanderer," said Oberon. "Take part of the flower, and seek through this grove. A sweet Athenian lady was here, who is in love with a **disdainful** youth. When you find him sleeping, drop some of the flower's love juice into his eyes. But do it when she is near him, so that she may be the first thing he sees when he awakes."

disdainful: disrespectful, full of dislike

"Fear not, my lord!" cried Puck. "Your servant shall do so!" And away he zipped.

Oberon went to seek the queen in her fairy **bower**. He found Titania preparing to rest on a bank of wildflowers.

bower: a pleasant shady place; or, a lady's private room

"Come," Titania was saying to her fairies, "sing me to sleep." The fairies sang a gentle lullaby, and as their queen drifted into sleep, they slipped away into the moonlight.

Unseen, Oberon softly drew near and dropped some of the love juice on Titania's eyelids, saying,

"What thou seest when thou dost wake,
Do it for thy true love take.

In thy eye, that shall appear
When thou wak'st, it is thy dear:
Wake when some **vile** thing is near."

vile: extremely unpleasant, offensive, disgusting

4

While all this was taking place, Hermia sneaked out of her father's house and ran to the wood. There she met Lysander, who was waiting to guide her to his aunt's house. Off they went through the moonlit shadows. But before they had passed through half the wood, they became so tired that they could go no farther. Lysander persuaded her to rest till morning on a bank of soft moss in a small **clearing**. Then, on the other side of the clearing, he found a place to lie down, and soon they were both asleep.

Puck soon appeared in the clearing where Hermia and Lysander slept. He grinned, as he was sure that this must be the **scornful** young man Oberon had sent him to find. He squeezed some of the love juice from the flower onto Lysander's

clearing: an open space in a forest

scornful: full of feelings of dislike and disrespect

eyes. "So awake when I am gone," whispered Puck, "for I must now to Oberon."

As Puck vanished, Helena stepped into the clearing. She was exhausted from chasing after Demetrius. As she dragged her tired feet, she almost stumbled across the sleeping Lysander.

"Ah," she cried, "this is Lysander, lying on the ground! Is he dead or asleep?" Shaking him, she said, "Good sir, if you are alive, awake!"

Lysander opened his eyes and caught sight of Helena. The magical flower did its work. Lysander took her hand and said with great urgency, "Not Hermia, but Helena I love!"

Helena was confused. She knew that Lysander was pledged to marry Hermia. Then a thought struck her—Lysander must be making fun of her! "Oh," said Helena, "why was I born to be **mocked** and scorned by everyone? And now you, sir, pretend to love me?"

mocked: teased, made fun of

In great anger, Helena ran away. Lysander followed her, quite forgetful of Hermia, who was still asleep.

When Hermia awoke she was frightened

to find herself alone. She wandered through the wood, worried and afraid, not knowing what had become of Lysander or where to find him.

5

The moonlight shone on the hidden bower where Titania, the fairy queen, lay asleep. Into this part of the wood walked Peter Quince and his fellow workmen, eager to rehearse their play.

"Here's a marvelous convenient place for our rehearsal!" cried Quince. As the workmen walked around, each muttering his lines, and some making grand gestures with their hands and arms—especially Bottom—a grinning fairy looked down upon them.

"What **hempen homespuns** have we **swaggering** here?" said Puck. At this moment, Bottom strutted by, and Puck could not resist a little magical mischief. With a wink, he gave Bottom the head of a donkey!

hempen homespuns: roughly dressed people

swaggering: strutting, walking proudly and confidently

When Bottom turned back to his fellow

workmen, they screamed in horror and ran. Puck laughed and, invisible, he zipped after them, pinching their arms and legs.

"Why do you run away?" cried Bottom, who was unaware that his head had been

"Why do you run away?" cried Bottom.

transformed. "I see what you are up to," said Bottom. "You mean to make an ass of me, to frighten me! Well, I am not afraid! I will walk up and down here and sing."

> **transformed:** completely changed in appearance or shape

Bottom sang so loudly that he woke the fairy queen. Titania emerged from her bower and saw the donkey-headed man. The juice of the little purple flower did its magic. She cried out, "What angel wakes me from my flowery bed?" Then she wrapped her arms around Bottom and whispered into his large donkey ear, "I love you. Go with me, and I will give you fairies to attend upon you."

With fairies flitting about him, Bottom followed the queen to her bower.

6

By this time, Puck had returned to Oberon. The mischievous sprite told the fairy king how he had found the group of workmen rehearsing in the wood, how he had given Bottom the head of a donkey, and how he had chased all the other workmen away, leaving Bottom alone with the sleeping fairy queen. "When in that moment," Puck concluded, "so it came to pass, Titania waked and **straightway** loved an ass!"

straightway (an old form of the word *straightaway*): at once, right away, immediately

Oberon laughed, pleased that his plan to get back at Titania had worked out even better than he had hoped. Then Oberon asked Puck if he had also charmed the eyes of the Athenian youth who had been mean to Helena. Puck assured Oberon that he had indeed put the magical flower juice on the young man's eyes.

Suddenly there was the sound of voices approaching. With a quick gesture, Oberon made himself and Puck invisible. Into the clearing ran Demetrius, followed by Hermia, both out of breath.

"Stand close," whispered Oberon to Puck. "This is the Athenian youth whose eyes I **bid** you charm."

bid: requested, ordered

Puck was puzzled. "This is the woman," he said, "but not this the man."

Oberon and Puck listened as Demetrius pledged his love to Hermia, while Hermia responded with anger. She was still searching for Lysander, and in her **desperation**, she imagined that Demetrius might have done something terrible to get rid of Lysander.

desperation: a state of hopelessness and extreme discouragement

slain: killed

"Hast thou **slain** Lysander in his sleep?" she cried to Demetrius.

"I am not guilty of Lysander's blood!" Demetrius said firmly.

Hermia **glared** at him and then ran away to continue her search for Lysander. Demetrius, frustrated and exhausted, decided that it would be useless to follow her. He lay down and fell fast asleep.

glared: stared angrily

Oberon, who now realized Puck's mistake, turned to his **sprite** and said, "Go now, find Helena, and bring her here."

sprite: fairy

In a flash, Puck went in search of Helena, while Oberon leaned over Demetrius and touched the sleeping youth's eyelids with the magic flower. Just then Puck reappeared to report, "Helena is here at hand."

Oberon and his sprite hurried away. At

this very moment Helena came running into the clearing, with Lysander close behind, vowing his love for her. Helena turned away and nearly fell over Demetrius, who woke with a start and caught sight of her. "O Helena," he sighed, "goddess, **nymph**, perfect, divine!"

nymph: in mythology, a nature spirit in the form of a beautiful girl

Helena was amazed. She looked back and forth between Lysander and Demetrius, who both praised her charms and vowed their love for her. Then her eyes turned dark as she understood what was happening—or so she believed—and she accused both men of cruelly making fun of her. "You both are **rivals**, and love Hermia," she cried, "and now both rivals, to mock Helena!"

rivals: competitors

Suddenly Hermia ran into the clearing, and, relieved, threw herself upon Lysander. But he pushed her away, as though she were some slimy and disgusting creature. Hermia stood amazed and confused. But she was even more amazed when Helena turned and accused Hermia of being part of the young men's plot to make fun of her.

"Hermia," Helena sniffed, "it is not kind to join with men in **scorning** your poor friend."

scorning: feeling extreme dislike and disrespect; treating someone as worthless

"I do not scorn you," answered Hermia, "but it seems that you scorn me."

As Helena and Hermia exchanged angry words, Demetrius and Lysander argued over which of them loved Helena the most. Their words became so heated that they slipped away into the wood to fight each other for Helena's love. When the women discovered that the men had left them, they once more wandered wearily into the wood to search for them.

As soon as they were gone, Oberon—who, with Puck, had been listening to their quarrels—turned to his sprite and said sternly, "This is thy **negligence**."

negligence: carelessness

To which Puck replied, "Believe me, king of shadows, I mistook."

"You saw," said the fairy king, "that Demetrius and Lysander are gone to seek a place to fight." To prevent this fight, Oberon ordered Puck to create a thick fog so that the **quarrelsome** lovers

quarrelsome: argumentative

would not be able to find each other in the dark. Then the fairy king told Puck to gather the four young lovers all in the same place, where they would be so weary that they would instantly fall asleep. Oberon gave Puck a second magical flower, and told the sprite to drop the juice of this other flower on Lysander's eyes, so that he would forget his new love for Helena and return to his old passion for Hermia.

Puck quickly set about his work, while Oberon went to see what had happened with the fairy queen.

7

Oberon soon found Titania and quietly spied on her. He listened as the fairy queen sighed to donkey-headed Bottom, "Come, let me kiss thy fair large ears, my gentle joy!"

"Where is Peaseblossom?" asked Bottom, very pleased with his new fairy attendants.

"Ready!" answered little Peaseblossom.

"Scratch my head," said Bottom. As

Peaseblossom and other fairies gently scratched his head, Bottom said, "I must to the barber's, for methinks I am marvelous hairy about the face."

"Sweet love," said the fairy queen, "what will you have to eat?"

"Truly, I could munch your good dry oats," said Bottom, who had gotten a donkey's appetite with his donkey's head. "But, let none of your people disturb me, for I have a mind to sleep."

"Sleep," said the fairy queen, "and I will wind you in my arms. Oh, how I love thee! How I dote on thee!"

When Oberon saw the donkey-headed man sleeping in the arms of Titania, he began to pity the fairy queen. He dropped some of the juice of the other flower onto her eyes and spoke these words:

> "**Be as thou wast wont to be**;
> See as thou wast wont to see:
> Now, my Titania; wake you,
> my sweet queen."

Be as thou wast wont to be: Be as you usually are

The fairy queen shook her head, as though

Sleep had quieted Helena's angry spirits.

she were coming out of a dream. She was alarmed at the sight of Bottom, but Oberon calmed her. Then the fairy king ordered Puck to remove the donkey head from Bottom. Puck did so and left Bottom sleeping peacefully.

"Come, my queen," said Oberon to Titania. Hand in loving hand, they led their fairy followers away before the coming dawn.

Not far away, Demetrius, Lysander, Hermia, and Helena were sleeping on the grass, where Puck, in the dense magical fog, had managed to bring them all to the same spot, unaware of each other. And he had carefully removed the charm from the eyes of Lysander.

Hermia awoke first and saw her lost Lysander asleep near her. Lysander then opened his eyes, which were no longer clouded by the fairy charm. He saw Hermia and smiled, and she knew that he had recovered his love for her.

Helena and Demetrius were by this time awake. Sleep had quieted Helena's angry spirits, so she listened with delight as Demetrius **affirmed** his love for her.

affirmed: stated strongly

They began to talk over the adventures of the night. They wondered whether these strange things had really happened, or if they had all been dreaming the same **bewildering** dream. All the unkind words that had passed among them were forgiven.

bewildering: extremely confusing, puzzling

As they prepared to return to Athens, they were all surprised at the sight of Egeus, Hermia's father, who had come to the wood as part of a hunting party led by Duke Theseus.

When Egeus saw Hermia hand in hand with Lysander, he cried out to Theseus, "Enough, enough, my lord! I beg the law upon them!"

But the duke—who was perhaps warmed by thoughts of his upcoming marriage to Hippolyta—said, "Egeus, I will overrule your will. In the temple, **by and by**, these couples shall **eternally be knit**."

by and by: in a little while
eternally be knit: forever be bound together (in marriage)

So the cruel sentence of death that had threatened Hermia was taken away, and instead she was happily married to Lysander. On the same day Helena was married to her beloved, the now faithful Demetrius. The wedding bells rang merrily throughout Athens.

At the evening's festivities to celebrate the marriage of Theseus to Hippolyta, as well as the weddings of the young lovers, the Athenian workmen performed their play about Pyramus and Thisbe. The effect of their performance was perhaps best summed up by Hippolyta, who remarked, "This is the silliest stuff that ever I heard!"

The fairy king and queen, who had together watched over the whole affair, were so delighted that they celebrated the weddings of these **mortals** by sports and revels throughout their fairy kingdom.

mortals: human beings

And now, if there are any who think this story of fairies and pranks is too strange to be true, they have only to think that they have been asleep and dreaming a harmless little midsummer night's dream.

William Shakespeare's
A Midsummer Night's Dream

An Abridged Version of the Play Adapted for Readers' Theater or Classroom Performance

This version of William Shakespeare's *A Midsummer Night's Dream* generally uses the original language, with a few words changed and a few lines moved. It has been shortened to make it practical for production in elementary or middle schools. It can also be enjoyed as a readers' theater or classroom performance.

Most of the stage directions *[the notes in brackets, like this]* are not Shakespeare's but have been written for this condensed version of the play. Some of these notes offer suggestions for staging a performance or for the actors' interpretation of dialogue.

This script adds three Speakers to Shakespeare's cast of characters. They serve to guide the audience through the play, to summarize the parts of the action that have been cut or condensed, and occasionally to clarify and comment on the action.

The script is printed on the left-hand pages, with some words underlined. You will find definitions of these underlined words on the right-hand pages.

Titania and her fairies with the transformed Bottom

A Note on Poetry and Prose

As you read through the script, you will notice that Shakespeare wrote some lines as poetry and some as prose. What's the difference?

Prose is everyday language. It is the language we usually speak and write. In Shakespeare's plays, everyday characters—such as the group of workmen in *A Midsummer Night's Dream*—speak in prose. For example, Nick Bottom, a weaver, speaks in prose to his friend, Peter Quince:

> First, good Peter Quince, say what the play is about, then read the names of the actors.

Except for the group of workmen in *A Midsummer Night's Dream*, the other characters speak in poetry. These characters are noble people, such as kings and queens, or people of high social position, or special characters like the inhabitants of the land of fairies. For example, a fairy called Puck speaks in poetry to another fairy:

> The king doth keep his revels here tonight.
> Take heed the queen come not within his sight!

Notice that each new line of poetry begins with a capital letter. As you read the lines of poetry aloud, you will feel a rhythm in them—often, it's a regular beat, like this: da DUM / da DUM / da DUM / da DUM / da DUM. In speaking the lines, you should not emphasize the beats—that would make the lines sound "sing-songy." Instead, just feel the rhythm and speak the words naturally.

Puck's two lines rhyme: *tonight/sight*. Sometimes Shakespeare's poetry rhymes, and sometimes it doesn't. For example, here a young woman named Hermia speaks to Duke Theseus:

> And I beseech your grace that I may know
> The worst that may befall me in this case,
> If I refuse to wed Demetrius.

Those lines are poetry, even though they don't rhyme. And, even though there is a break between the first two lines, there is no comma or other punctuation mark. So, in speaking these lines, you would not pause between them. Instead, you would just keep going, like this: ". . . that I may know the worst that may befall me in this case . . ."

Whether the lines are prose or poetry, just speak them naturally—that's the key.

CHARACTERS IN THE PLAY

At the Duke's court
THESEUS (/**thee**•see•us/), duke of Athens
HIPPLOYTA (/hih•**pol**•ih•tuh/), queen of the Amazons,
    about to be wedded to Theseus
EGEUS (/ee•**gee**•us/), father to Hermia
PHILOSTRATE (/**fill**•oh•straet/), a courtier in service of Theseus

The four young lovers
HERMIA (/**her**•mee•uh/), daughter of Egeus, in love
    with Lysander
HELENA* (/**hel**•en•uh/), in love with Demetrius
LYSANDER (/lie •**san**•der/), in love with Hermia
DEMETRIUS (/dih•**mee**•tree•us/), who wants to marry Hermia

The workmen of Athens
PETER QUINCE, a carpenter who directs their play
NICK BOTTOM, a weaver who plays Pyramus
FRANCIS FLUTE, a bellows-mender who plays Thisbe
TOM SNOUT, a tinker who plays the Wall
SNUG, a joiner who plays the Lion
ROBIN STARVELING, a tailor who plays Moonshine

In Fairy Land
TITANIA (/tih•**tahn**•yuh/), queen of the fairies
OBERON (/**oh**•bur•on/), king of the fairies
PUCK, also known as Robin Goodfellow, a mischievous
    hobgoblin in service to Oberon
PEASEBLOSSOM, a fairy attending upon Titania
COBWEB, a fairy attending upon Titania
MOTH, a fairy attending upon Titania
MUSTARDSEED, a fairy attending upon Titania

Amazons: In Greek mythology, the Amazons were a tribe of women warriors.

courtier: an advisor or assistant to a king or queen or other person of royalty

*In assigning roles, note that in Act 3 Scene 2, Helena is described as taller than Hermia.

bellows-mender: one whose job is to repair a bellows, a tool, often made of leather and wood, that blows air when squeezed

tinker: one who repairs household items that are made of metal

joiner: a kind of carpenter or furniture-maker

hobgoblin: a mischievous imp

ACT 1

SCENE 1: ATHENS, THE PALACE OF DUKE THESEUS.

[*Enter SPEAKERS 1, 2, and 3.*]

SPEAKER 1 [*enthusiastically*]
Ladies and gentlemen, welcome to our play!

SPEAKER 2
You'll meet the actors in a minute.

SPEAKER 3
We're here to help tell the story—the story of William Shakespeare's . . .

ALL
A Midsummer Night's Dream!

SPEAKER 1
Once upon a time . . .

SPEAKER 2
In the city of Athens . . .

SPEAKER 3
There was a very strict law.

SPEAKER 1
This law said that a daughter must marry the man her father chose for her.

SPEAKER 2
And if the daughter refused to marry the man her father had chosen . . .

SPEAKER 3
Then she could be put to death!

SPEAKER 1
That's terrible!

SPEAKER 2
That's wrong!

SPEAKER 3
That's crazy!

SPEAKER 1
But don't worry—it's not real.

SPEAKER 2
It's only make-believe.

SPEAKER 3
But it's real in the make-believe world of our play . . . if you get what I'm saying.

Act 1, Scene 1

SPEAKER 1
Oh, right, our play! One day, in the city of Athens...

SPEAKER 2
Duke Theseus was eagerly awaiting his wedding to the warrior queen Hippolyta.

[*Enter THESEUS and HIPPOLYTA, arm in arm.*]

SPEAKER 3
The wedding is just a few days away, but for Theseus, time seems to be moving too slowly.

THESEUS
Now, fair Hippolyta, our nuptial hour
Draws on apace. Four happy days bring in
Another moon. But, O, methinks how slow
This old moon wanes.

HIPPOLYTA [*moving away from THESEUS*]
Four days will quickly steep themselves in night;
Four nights will quickly dream away the time.

[*He takes her hands. While this is happening, the SPEAKERS comment:*]

nuptial hour: the time for a wedding

draws on apace: approaches quickly

methinks: it seems to me

wanes: grows smaller (or appears to)

steep themselves in: be absorbed or dissolved into

SPEAKER 1 [*in the tone used when you see a cute puppy*]
Awwwww!

SPEAKER 2
That's so sweet!

SPEAKER 3
I love a wedding! [*sniffs, dabs eyes*]

[*Suddenly, EGEUS stomps in, with his daughter, HERMIA, behind him.*]

EGEUS [*bowing to THESEUS*]
Happy be Theseus, our renownèd duke!

SPEAKER 1
Ouch—way to break the mood!

SPEAKER 2
That's old Egeus—and he looks pretty angry.

SPEAKER 3
And his daughter doesn't look too happy either.

THESEUS [*annoyed, making an effort to be courteous*]
Thanks, good Egeus. What's the news with thee?

[*EGEUS signals for DEMETRIUS and LYSANDER, who enter promptly, bow to the duke, and stand aside.*]

renownèd: famous, celebrated

Pronunciation Note: The grave accent mark indicates that the normally silent vowel is pronounced (to keep the rhythm in the poetic line). So, "renownèd" is spoken as three syllables: re•nown•ed.

EGEUS
Full of vexation come I, with complaint
Against my child, my daughter Hermia.
Stand forth, Demetrius.
[*DEMETRIUS steps forward smugly.*]
    My noble lord,
This man hath my consent to marry her.
Stand forth, Lysander.
[*Lysander steps forward defiantly.*]
    And, my gracious duke,
This man hath bewitched the bosom of my child.
Thou, Lysander, hath warped my daughter's heart,
Turned her obedience, which is due to me,
To stubborn harshness. And, my gracious duke,
If my daughter will not here before your grace
Consent to marry with Demetrius,
I beg the ancient privilege of Athens.
As she is mine, I may dispose of her,
Which shall be either to this gentleman
Or to her death, according to our law!

[*HIPPOLYTA gasps in horror.*]

THESEUS
What say you, Hermia?
Demetrius is a worthy gentleman.

vexation: the state of being worried and annoyed

hath: has

bosom: heart

dispose of her: give her away; deal with her

HERMIA
So is Lysander.
I do entreat your grace to pardon me.
And I beseech your grace that I may know
The worst that may befall me in this case,
If I refuse to wed Demetrius.

THESEUS
Either to die the death or to give up
Forever the society of men.*

[*HIPPOLYTA, upset, steps away from THESEUS.*]

DEMETRIUS
Relent, sweet Hermia. And, Lysander, yield.

LYSANDER
You have her father's love, Demetrius;
Let me have Hermia's. Do you marry him!**

EGEUS
Scornful Lysander!

LYSANDER
I am beloved of beauteous Hermia.
[Pointing at DEMETRIUS]
He courted Nedar's daughter, Helena,
And she devoutly dotes upon this man!

entreat: ask, plead, beg

your grace: a respectful way of referring to a person of royalty, such as Theseus

beseech: beg; ask urgently

befall me: happen to me

* Theseus is saying that if Hermia refuses to marry the man her father has chosen, then she must die or live apart from society as a kind of nun.

relent: give way, back down, change one's mind

yield: give up, admit defeat

** "Do you marry him!" is a command, not a question. Lysander is mocking Demetrius by telling him to marry Egeus.

scornful: full of feelings of dislike and disrespect

courted: tried to win the affection of (with the intention of marrying)

devoutly dotes upon: devotedly shows excessive affection for

[DEMETRIUS and LYSANDER approach each other threateningly, but are stopped by the Duke's voice.]

THESEUS
Demetrius, come!
And come, Egeus. You shall go with me.
For you, fair Hermia, look you arm yourself
To fit your fancies to your father's will,
Or else the law of Athens yields you up
To death, or to a vow of single life.
Come, my Hippolyta.

[HIPPOLYTA turns on her heel and exits briskly. THESEUS, flustered, follows her. Behind him follow EGEUS and DEMETRIUS, leaving LYSANDER and HERMIA alone.]

LYSANDER
Ay me!
The course of true love never did run smooth.

HERMIA
Alas! To choose love by another's eyes!

LYSANDER *[excited by a sudden idea]*
Hear me, Hermia.

[He takes her hand and pulls her aside. They mime* as the SPEAKERS explain that. . .]

arm yourself: prepare yourself

fit your fancies: shape your wishes

ay (pronounced "eye"): an expression of sorrow or distress

alas: an expression of sadness

> * While the Speakers summarize the action, the actors may silently enact what the Speakers are describing.

SPEAKER 1
Lysander has a plan!

SPEAKER 2
He tells Hermia that he has an aunt who lives miles away from Athens.

SPEAKER 3
He urges her to run away with him to where his aunt lives.

SPEAKER 1
Because there, away from the city, the cruel law of Athens does not apply.

SPEAKER 2
Which means—they can get married!

SPEAKER 3
Lysander tells Hermia to sneak away tomorrow night, and meet him in the wood outside town.

LYSANDER
Therefore, hear me, Hermia. If thou lovest me,
Steal forth thy father's house tomorrow night;
And in the wood, a league without the town,
Where I did meet thee once with Helena,
There will I stay for thee.

steal forth: sneak away from

league: a distance of a few miles

stay: wait

HERMIA
My good Lysander!
I swear to thee, by Cupid's strongest bow,
Tomorrow truly will I meet with thee.

LYSANDER
Keep promise, love. Look, here comes Helena.

[*Enter HELENA. Actors freeze as SPEAKERS explain that...*]

SPEAKER 1
Helena has been Hermia's best friend since they were little.

SPEAKER 2
But now Helena is feeling sad. Because she loves Demetrius...

SPEAKER 3
But Demetrius doesn't love Helena. He wants to marry Hermia.

HERMIA
God speed, fair Helena!

HELENA
Call you me "fair"? That fair again unsay.
Demetrius loves your fair. O happy fair!

Act 1, Scene 1

Cupid: In mythology, Cupid is a god of love who carries a bow and arrows. The arrows fill a person with love for another person.

God speed: a greeting expressing good wishes

unsay: take back what was said

HERMIA
I frown upon him, yet he loves me still.

HELENA
O that your frowns would teach my smiles such skill!

HERMIA
The more I hate, the more he follows me.

HELENA
The more I love, the more he hateth me.

HERMIA
Take comfort. He no more shall see my face;
Lysander and myself will fly this place.

LYSANDER
Tomorrow night,
Through Athens's gates have we devised to steal.

HERMIA
And in the wood, where often you and I
Upon faint primrose beds were wont to lie,
There my Lysander and myself shall meet.
Farewell, sweet playfellow. Pray thou for us.
And good luck grant thee thy Demetrius!

[*Exit HERMIA and LYSANDER.*]

fly: run away from, flee

devised to steal: planned to sneak away

faint primrose beds: gently scented beds of pale, yellow flowers

wont to: used to, accustomed to

farewell: goodbye

grant thee: give you

HELENA
How happy some o'er other some can be!
Through Athens I am thought as fair as she.
But what of that? Demetrius thinks not so.
Before Demetrius looked on Hermia's eyes,
He hailed down oaths that he was only mine.
[*She has a sudden idea.*]
I will go tell him of fair Hermia's flight!
Then to the wood will he tomorrow night.
And for this intelligence, I will have thanks!

[*Exit HELENA.*]

SPEAKER 1
There goes jealous Helena, rushing to tell Demetrius that Hermia and Lysander are sneaking away to get married.

SPEAKER 2
For this, she hopes Demetrius will love her again. Will he? We'll soon find out.

SPEAKER 3
But now our scene shifts to a small cottage in Athens, where six workmen have gathered.

[*Enter QUINCE, SNUG, BOTTOM, FLUTE, SNOUT, and STARVELING.*]

o'er other some: over (in comparison to) some other person

hailed down oaths: made many promises

flight: running away

intelligence: important information

SPEAKER 1
As part of the festivities to celebrate the marriage of the Duke to Hippolyta, these workmen are planning to put on a play.

SPEAKER 2
Wait—these guys are in our play, but they're also planning to put on a play?

SPEAKER 3
So—it's a play within a play.

ALL 3 [*in a tone that says, "Now I get it"*]
Ohhhhhhh. . .

SCENE 2: ATHENS, PETER QUINCE'S HOUSE.

QUINCE
Is all our company here?

BOTTOM [*who likes to give advice*]
You were best to call them man by man.

QUINCE
Here is the scroll of every man's name thought fit, through all Athens, to play in our interlude before the duke and the duchess, on their wedding day at night.

scroll: list

interlude: a short play

BOTTOM [*explaining the "right" way to begin*]
First, good Peter Quince, say what the play is about, then read the names of the actors.

QUINCE
Our play is, *The Most Lamentable Comedy and Most Cruel Death of Pyramus and Thisbe.*

BOTTOM
A very good piece of work, I assure you. Now, good Peter Quince, call forth your actors by the scroll. Masters, spread yourselves.

QUINCE
Answer as I call you. Nick Bottom, the weaver.

BOTTOM
Ready. Name what part I am for, and proceed.

QUINCE
You, Nick Bottom, are set down for Pyramus.

BOTTOM
What is Pyramus? A lover, or a tyrant?

QUINCE
A lover, that kills himself most gallant for love.

lamentable: sorrowful

Pyramus and Thisbe: the main characters in a tragic love story from ancient mythology

tyrant: a cruel ruler

most gallant: in a very noble, self-sacrificing way

BOTTOM
That will ask some tears in the true performing of it.
If I do it, I will move storms.
[Taking center stage, he overdoes it mightily.]
>The raging rocks
>And shivering shocks
>Shall break the locks
>Of prison gates!

[He resumes his place, very pleased with himself.]
This was lofty! Now name the rest of the players.

QUINCE
Francis Flute, the bellows-mender.

FLUTE
Here, Peter Quince.

QUINCE
Flute, you must take Thisbe on you.

FLUTE
What is Thisbe? A wandering knight?

QUINCE
It is the lady that Pyramus must love.

[The other workmen snicker and tease FLUTE.]

FLUTE
Nay, let me not play a woman! I have a beard coming.

nay: no

QUINCE
You shall play it in a mask, and you may speak as small as you will.

BOTTOM [*jumping in impulsively*]
Let me play Thisbe too! I'll speak in a monstrous little voice.
[*in a high and squeaky voice*]
Ah, Pyramus, lover dear!
Thy Thisbe dear, and lady dear!

QUINCE [*starting to lose patience*]
No, no. You must play Pyramus. And Flute, you Thisbe.

BOTTOM [*disappointed*]
Well, proceed.

QUINCE
Robin Starveling, the tailor.

STARVELING
Here, Peter Quince.

QUINCE
Robin Starveling, you must play Thisbe's mother. Tom Snout, the tinker.

SNOUT
Here, Peter Quince.

QUINCE
You, Pyramus's father. Myself, Thisbe's father. Snug, the joiner—you, the lion's part.

SNUG
Have you the lion's part written? Pray you, if it be, give it me, for I am slow of study.

QUINCE
It is nothing but roaring.

BOTTOM [*bursting with excitement*]
Let me play the lion too! I will roar, that it will do any man's heart good to hear me. [*roars loudly*] I will roar, that I will make the duke say, "Let him roar again. Let him roar again!"

QUINCE
If you should do it too terribly, you would frighten the duchess and the ladies.

BOTTOM
I will aggravate my voice so that I will roar you as gently as any dove or nightingale. [*He makes gentle purring, cooing sounds.*]

pray you: if you would, please

aggravate: to make worse (Bottom here misuses the word; he means the opposite, that he will soften his voice.)

QUINCE
You can play no part but Pyramus!
[*BOTTOM sulks. QUINCE tries to win him over.*]
For Pyramus is a sweet-faced man, a most lovely gentleman-like man. Therefore you must play Pyramus.

BOTTOM
Well... I will undertake it!

[*QUINCE hands out scripts to each workman.*]

QUINCE
Here are your parts. And I entreat you to learn them by tomorrow night, and meet me in the wood, a mile without the town, by moonlight. There will we rehearse. I pray you, fail me not.

BOTTOM
We will meet and rehearse most courageously!

[*A cheer as they exit.*]

entreat: beg, plead, request strongly

I pray you: I ask you; I urge you

ACT 2

SCENE 1: THE WOOD OUTSIDE ATHENS.

SPEAKER 1
There go the workmen, off to study their lines before they meet in the wood to rehearse.

SPEAKER 2
The same wood where Hermia and Lysander are meeting before they sneak away to get married . . . and where Helena has told Demetrius to find them.

SPEAKER 3
The same wood where, on a midsummer night, you might catch a glimpse of the fairies, singing and dancing and making mischief. Look!

[Enter PUCK and FAIRY from opposite directions.]

PUCK
How now, spirit? Whither wander you?

FAIRY*
Over hill, over dale,
Through bush, through brier,
Over park, over pale,
Through flood, through fire,

how now: what's going on?
whither: to what place

*This fairy may be one of the named fairies (Peaseblossom, Cobweb, Mustardseed, or Moth), or a distinct character played by a different actor.

dale: valley

pale: a fenced field

I do wander everywhere,
Swifter than the moon's sphere,
And I serve the fairy queen.

PUCK [*giving a warning*]
The king doth keep his revels here tonight.
Take heed the queen come not within his sight!

FAIRY
Either I mistake your shape and making quite,
Or else you are that shrewd and knavish sprite
Called Robin Goodfellow, and sweet Puck . . .

PUCK
Thou speak'st aright!
I am that merry wanderer of the night.
But room, fairy! Here comes Oberon.

FAIRY
And here my mistress. Would that he were gone!

[*Enter, from one side, the fairy king, OBERON; from the other, the fairy queen, TITANIA, accompanied by FAIRIES. PUCK rushes to OBERON, and the FAIRIES to TITANIA.*]

OBERON
Ill met by moonlight, proud Titania.

doth keep his revels: does hold his entertainments (such as sports or dancing)

take heed: pay careful attention (often said as a warning)

shrewd: mischievous

knavish: like a rascal or trickster

sprite: fairy

Thou speak'st aright: The words you speak are true.

room: make room, step aside

would that: I wish that

ill met: unhappily or unfortunately encountered

TITANIA
What, jealous Oberon! Fairies, skip hence.

OBERON
Tarry, rash wanton. Am not I thy lord?

TITANIA [*with a sarcastic edge*]
Then I must be thy lady.

[*They circle each other warily.*]

SPEAKER 1
All is not well in Fairyland.

SPEAKER 2
The fairy king and fairy queen are angry with each other.

SPEAKER 3
They are having a big argument about a little boy.

SPEAKER 1
The mother of this little boy was a lady devoted to Titania.

SPEAKER 2
But then this lady died, and so the fairy queen took the boy to the wood to care for him and raise him.

tarry: wait

rash wanton: impulsive, rebellious person

SPEAKER 3
But Oberon wanted the child for his own.

OBERON
Why should Titania <u>cross</u> her Oberon?
<u>I do but beg</u> a little <u>changeling</u> boy
To be my <u>henchman</u>.

TITANIA
Set your heart at rest:
The Fairyland buys not the child of me.*
His mother was a <u>vot'ress</u> of my order:
And, in the spicèd Indian air, by night,
<u>Full often</u> hath she <u>gossiped</u> by my side,
And sat with me on <u>Neptune's</u> yellow sands.
But she, being mortal, of that boy did die,**
And for her sake do I <u>rear up</u> her boy,
And for her sake I will not part with him.

OBERON [*commanding*]
Give me that boy!

TITANIA [*boldly*]
Not for thy fairy kingdom! Fairies, away!

[*Exit TITANIA and FAIRIES.*]

Act 2, Scene 1

cross: oppose, resist, defy

I do but beg: I only ask

changeling: a human child taken by the fairies; sometimes refers to a fairy child who is left by the fairies in place of a stolen human child

henchman: follower, assistant

> * Titania is saying that she will not give up the child for all of Fairyland.

vot'ress: a votaress, a devoted follower

full often: very often

gossiped: talked about this and that

Neptune: in mythology, the god of the sea

rear up: raise

> **The boy's mother died in childbirth.

OBERON
Well, go thy way.
I shall torment thee for this injury.
My gentle Puck, come hither.

[*PUCK scampers to OBERON's side.*]

Thou rememberest a little western flower
That maidens call love-in-idleness.
Fetch me that flower, the herb I showed thee once.
The juice of it on sleeping eyelids laid
Will make or man or woman madly dote
Upon the next live creature that it sees.
Fetch me this herb!

PUCK
I'll put a girdle round about the earth
In forty minutes!

[*Exit PUCK, speedily.*]

OBERON
Having once this juice,
I'll watch Titania when she is asleep,
And drop the liquor of it in her eyes.
The next thing then she waking looks upon,
Be it on lion, bear, or wolf, or bull,
On meddling monkey, or on busy ape,
She shall pursue it with the soul of love.

torment: to cause pain or distress

injury: hurtful act

hither: here, to this place

thou rememberest: you remember; you recall

or man or woman: either man or woman

dote upon: to show excessive affection and attention

put a girdle round about the earth: circle the earth

having once: as soon as I have

liquor: liquid

And <u>ere</u> I take this charm from off her sight,
As I can take it with another herb,
I'll make her <u>render up</u> the boy to me.

[*A noise comes from offstage—it could be HELENA crying, "Wait! Wait!"*]

But who comes here? I am invisible!

[*He steps aside, invisible.*]

SPEAKER 1
So, Oberon has sent Puck to bring him a magical flower.

SPEAKER 2
A flower that can make you fall in love with the first thing you see.

SPEAKER 3
And Oberon plans to use the flower to cast a spell on Titania.

SPEAKER 1 [*worried*]
I have a bad feeling about this.

SPEAKER 2 [*reassuring*]
But there's another flower that can undo the spell.

ere: before

render up: hand over

SPEAKER 3
Shhh—look who's coming into the wood!

[*DEMETRIUS enters, looking for someone.*]

SPEAKER 1
It's Demetrius. He's searching for Hermia and Lysander.

SPEAKER 2
Helena told him about their plan to meet in the wood and run away to get married.

SPEAKER 3
By telling Demetrius their secret, Helena thinks she will win his heart. Will she?

[*HELENA enters, gasping, clutching at DEMETRIUS. He brushes her away. OBERON, invisible, watches them.*]

DEMETRIUS
I love thee not, therefore pursue me not.
Where is Lysander? And fair Hermia?

[*HELENA reaches for DEMETRIUS. Again he brushes her aside.*]

Hence, get thee gone, and follow me no more!
Do I not in plainest truth tell you
That I do not, nor I cannot love you?

hence: go away

HELENA
And even for that do I love you the more.
I am your spaniel! Only give me leave,
Unworthy as I am, to follow you.

[*HELENA stares at DEMETRIUS, making big, sad, puppy-like eyes.*]

DEMETRIUS [*moving away from her*]
I am sick when I do look on thee.

HELENA [*moving toward him*]
And I am sick when I look not on you.

DEMETRIUS
I'll run from thee and hide me!

[*Exit DEMETRIUS, running.*]

HELENA
I'll follow thee!

[*Exit HELENA, running after DEMETRIUS.*]

OBERON [*stepping forward, now visible*]
Fare thee well, nymph. Ere he do leave this grove,
He shall seek thy love.

[*Enter PUCK.*]

Welcome, wanderer. Hast thou the flower there?

spaniel: loyal dog

give me leave: allow me

nymph: in mythology, a nature spirit in the form of a beautiful, young girl

ere he do leave: before he leaves

PUCK [*handing over the flower*]
Ay, here it is.

OBERON
I know a bank where the wild thyme blows,
Where oxlips and the nodding violet grows—
There sleeps Titania sometime of the night,
Lulled in these flowers with dances and delight.
And with the juice of this I'll streak her eyes,
And make her full of hateful fantasies.

[*PUCK laughs with mischievous glee. OBERON hands PUCK part of the flower.*]

Take thou some of it, and seek through this grove.
A sweet Athenian lady is in love
With a disdainful youth. Anoint his eyes,
But do it when the next thing he espies
May be the lady.

PUCK
Fear not, my lord, your servant shall do so!

[*Exit PUCK one way and OBERON another.*]

SPEAKER 1
So, Oberon is on his way to use the magic flower to cast a spell on Titania.

ay (pronounced "eye"): yes

thyme: a low-growing plant with strongly scented flowers

blows: blossoms

oxlips: a flowering plant, usually with yellow flowers

nodding: bending downward

lulled: soothed, relaxed

of this: of the magic flower

hateful fantasies: horrible visions

disdainful: scornful

anoint: rub with oil [in this case, the liquid of the magic flower]

espies: sees

SPEAKER 2
And Puck is on his way to use the flower to make Demetrius fall in love with Helena.

SPEAKER 3
Now it's nighttime, and Titania is getting ready to sleep in her bed of flowers.

SCENE 2: ANOTHER PART OF THE WOOD.

[*Enter TITANIA and FAIRIES.*]

TITANIA [*lying down*]
Come, a fairy song. Sing me now to sleep.

FAIRIES [*singing*]
You spotted snakes with double tongue,
Thorny hedgehogs, be not seen;
Newts and blind-worms, do no wrong,
Come not near our fairy queen.
Lulla, lulla, lullaby . . .

[*Exit FAIRIES, singing.*]

Lulla, lulla, lullaby.

[*Enter OBERON, sneakily. He squeezes the flower over the sleeping TITANIA's eyes.*]

OBERON
What thou seest when thou dost wake,
Do it for thy true love take.
In thy eye, that shall appear
When thou wakest, it is thy dear:
Wake when some vile thing is near.

[*Exit OBERON. TITANIA remains sleeping.*]

SPEAKER 1
While all this fairy mischief has been going on . . .

SPEAKER 2
Hermia has sneaked out of her father's house and run away to the wood.

[*Enter HERMIA, looking around eagerly. She does not notice TITANIA.*]

SPEAKER 3
She's meeting Lysander, who intends to guide her to his aunt's house, miles away from Athens.

[*Enter LYSANDER, who happily takes HERMIA by the hand.*]

what thou seest: whatever you see

that shall appear / When thou wakest: whatever appears when you wake up

vile: extremely unpleasant, offensive, disgusting

SPEAKER 1
Off they go through the moonlit shadows.

SPEAKER 2
But it's hard to make their way through the dense, dark wood.

[*LYSANDER and HERMIA mime pulling back branches, stumbling, etc. They do not see TITANIA.*]

SPEAKER 3
Soon, they are both tired and lost.

LYSANDER [*catching his breath*]
We'll rest us, Hermia, if you think it good,
And tarry for the comfort of the day.

HERMIA
Be it so, Lysander. Find you out a bed,
For I upon this bank will rest my head.

[*She lies down.*]

LYSANDER
Here is my bed. Sleep give thee all his rest!

[*He lies down away from her. They sleep.*]

Act 2, Scene 2

tarry: wait; stay in one place

[*Enter PUCK. At first he does not see LYSANDER or HERMIA.*]

PUCK [*frustrated*]
Through the forest have I gone,
But Athenian found I none.

[*He stumbles upon LYSANDER.*]

Who is here?
[*Excited*] This is he, my master said,
Despisèd the Athenian maid!

[*He sees HERMIA and scurries to her.*]

And here the maiden, sleeping sound,
On the dank and dirty ground.

[*He zips back to LYSANDER and squeezes the flower over his eyes.*]

Churl, upon thy eyes I throw
All the power this charm doth owe.
So awake when I am gone,
For I must now to Oberon.

[*Exit PUCK in a flash.*]

despisèd (pronounced as three syllables , de•spis•ed): hated, regarded with disgust

dank: damp

churl: a rude person

owe: own, possess

SPEAKER 1
Puck just put the magic flower juice in Lysander's eyes!

SPEAKER 2
But he was supposed to use it on Demetrius.

SPEAKER 3
Um, guys, speaking of Demetrius—

[*Enter DEMETRIUS and HELENA, running, gasping for breath. They do not see LYSANDER or HERMIA.*]

HELENA
Stay, sweet Demetrius!

DEMETRIUS
I charge thee, hence, and do not haunt me thus!

HELENA
O, wilt thou darkling leave me? Do not so.

DEMETRIUS
Stay! I alone will go.

[*Exit DEMETRIUS.*]

charge: command

darkling: in the dark

HELENA
O, I am out of breath in this fond chase!
Happy is Hermia, wherever she lies,
For she hath blessed and attractive eyes.
But oh, oh, I am as ugly as a bear,
For beasts that meet me run away for fear.

[*She bumps into the sleeping LYSANDER.*]

But who is here? Lysander! On the ground!
Dead? Or asleep? I see no blood, no wound.
Lysander if you live, good sir, awake.

[*She shakes him.*]

LYSANDER [*He wakes up, sees HELENA, and immediately falls in love with her.*]
And run through fire I will for thy sweet sake.
Transparent Helena! [*He looks around for DEMETRIUS.*]
Where is Demetrius? O, how fit a word
Is that vile name to perish on my sword!

HELENA
Do not say so. Lysander, say not so.
What though he love your Hermia? Lord, what though?
Yet Hermia still loves you. Then be content.

fond: foolish, silly

transparent: shining, radiant

LYSANDER
Content with Hermia! No, I do repent
The tedious minutes I with her have spent.
Not Hermia but Helena I love!
Who will not change a raven for a dove?

[*He reaches out to hug HELENA. For a very brief moment, she is thrilled that somebody loves her. But in a flash, her delight turns to a jealous suspicion that LYSANDER is making fun of her. She backs away from LYSANDER, saying:*]

HELENA
Wherefore was I to this keen mockery born?
When at your hands did I deserve this scorn?
Good troth, you do me wrong, good sooth, you do,
In such disdainful manner me to woo.
But fare you well! Perforce I must confess
I thought you lord of more true gentleness.

[*Exit HELENA in angry rush.*]

LYSANDER [*turning to the sleeping HERMIA*]
Hermia, sleep thou there,
And never mayst thou come Lysander near!
[*turning to where HELENA just left*]
And, all my powers, address your love and might
To honor Helen and to be her knight!

tedious: boring, dull

wherefore: why, for what reason

keen: sharp, bitter

mockery: teasing, making fun of

scorn: extreme dislike and disrespect; the feeling or belief that someone is worthless

good troth: an expression meaning something like "by my word" or "upon my oath"

good sooth: an expression meaning "truly, in truth"

to woo: to try to win someone's affection

perforce: of necessity

gentleness: courtesy, good manners

mayst thou: may you

[*Exit LYSANDER, leaving HERMIA alone. She stirs, disturbed by a bad dream.*]

HERMIA [*waking with a cry*]
Help me, Lysander, help me! Do thy best
To pluck this crawling serpent from my breast!
Ay me, for pity! What a dream was here!
Lysander! [*She looks around.*] Lysander!
[*With growing panic, she rises.*]
What, gone? No sound, no word?
Alack, where are you? Speak!

[*Exit HERMIA, frightened, seeking LYSANDER.*]

Act 2, Scene 2

serpent: snake

alack: an exclamation of sorrow or dismay

ACT 3

SCENE 1: THE WOOD, TITANIA LYING ASLEEP.

SPEAKER 1
There goes Hermia, chasing after Lysander.

SPEAKER 2
But she doesn't know that Lysander is under a spell and chasing after Helena!

SPEAKER 3
While Helena herself is chasing after Demetrius!

SPEAKER 1
And here lies the fairy queen, Titania, deeply asleep.

SPEAKER 2
Her eyes have also been charmed by the magic flower juice.

SPEAKER 3
I wonder what will be the first thing she sees when she wakes up?

[Enter BOTTOM, followed by the other workmen.]

BOTTOM
Are we all met?

QUINCE
Here's a marvelous convenient place for our rehearsal!

BOTTOM [*with excessively serious concern*]
Peter Quince! There are things in this comedy of Pyramus and Thisbe that will never please. First, Pyramus must draw a sword to kill himself, which the ladies cannot abide.

[*The other workmen whisper and worry.*]

STARVELING
I believe we must leave the killing out, when all is done.

BOTTOM [*eagerly*]
Not a whit! I have a device to make all well. Write me a prologue! And let the prologue seem to say, we will do no harm with our swords, and that Pyramus is not killed indeed. And, tell them that I, Pyramus, am not Pyramus, but Bottom the weaver. This will put them out of fear.

[*The workmen nod and express their approval.*]

all met: all here, all in attendance

cannot abide: cannot stand or put up with

when all is done: after all

whit: bit

device: plan

prologue: a speech spoken by an actor directly to the audience to introduce a play

QUINCE
Well, we will have such a prologue.

SNOUT
Will not the ladies be afeard of the lion?

STARVELING
I fear it, I promise you.

BOTTOM
Masters, to bring in a lion among ladies, is a most dreadful thing, for there is not a more fearful wild-fowl* than your lion living!

SNOUT [*having a bright idea*]
Therefore another prologue must tell he is not a lion.

BOTTOM
Nay, he himself must name his name, saying thus: "Ladies—or, fair ladies, I would wish you not to fear, not to tremble. You may think I come hither as a lion—but I am no such thing"—and there indeed let him tell them plainly he is Snug the joiner.

QUINCE
Well, it shall be so. [*suddenly worried*] But there are two hard things—first, to bring in the moonlight, for, you know, Pyramus and Thisbe meet by moonlight.

Act 3, Scene 1

afeard: afraid

* As he often does, Bottom is misusing a word here, as a "fowl" is a bird.

BOTTOM
Why, you must leave a window open in the great chamber, where we play, and the moon may shine in.

QUINCE [*doubtfully*]
Ay; or [*excited*] one must come in with a lantern, and say he comes to present the person of Moonshine!

[*murmurs of approval*]

Then, there is another thing.

[*worried murmuring*]

We must have a wall in the great chamber—for Pyramus and Thisbe, says the story, did talk through the chink of a wall.

SNOUT [*discouraged*]
You can never bring in a wall. What say you, Bottom?

BOTTOM
[*There is a brief, suspenseful pause as BOTTOM strokes his chin, furrows his brow, then gets an inspired idea.*]
Some man or other must present Wall! And let him have some plaster about him to signify "wall"; and let him hold his fingers thus, and through that cranny shall Pyramus and Thisbe whisper.

Act 3, Scene 1

chamber: meeting room

to present the person of: to play the character of

chink: a small crack or opening

present: play the part of

signify: indicate

cranny: a narrow opening

[*The workmen nod, cheer, and applaud.*]

QUINCE
Then all is well! Come, sit down, and rehearse your parts. Pyramus, you begin.

[*As BOTTOM takes center stage and the other workmen move aside, PUCK enters.*]

PUCK
What hempen homespuns have we swaggering here, so near the cradle of the fairy queen?

[*He grins mischievously and watches the workmen, who do not see him.*]

QUINCE
Speak, Pyramus. Thisbe, stand forth.

[*FLUTE stands sullenly apart; BOTTOM takes him by the hand and pulls him into the scene.*]

BOTTOM [*in a booming, super-romantic voice*]
My dearest Thisbe dear!

[*FLUTE winces and tries to pull away; BOTTOM holds on even tighter.*]

Stay thou but here awhile, and by and by I will to thee appear!

hempen homespuns: roughly dressed people

swaggering: strutting, walking proudly

by and by: in a little while

[*Exit BOTTOM, striding like a romantic hero.*]

PUCK
A stranger Pyramus than e'er played here.

[*Exit PUCK, following BOTTOM.*]

FLUTE [*whining*]
Must I speak now?

QUINCE
Ay, you must!

FLUTE [*attempting a high girlish voice*]
Most radiant Pyramus . . .

[*The others laugh and whoop. FLUTE glares at them.*]

I'll meet thee, Pyramus, at Ninny's tomb.

QUINCE
Ninus's tomb, man!

[*QUINCE looks around for BOTTOM.*]

Pyramus, enter! Your cue is past!

[*Enter PUCK, smiling and leading in BOTTOM, whose head PUCK has magically changed into a donkey's head—though BOTTOM doesn't know it.*]

Act 3, Scene 1

e'er: ever

Ninus's tomb: In the ancient myth, Pyramus and Thisbe agree to meet at the tomb of a king named Ninus *(/NYE•nus/)*.

cue: a word or action that signals an actor to begin his or her speech or performance

BOTTOM [*booming out his line*]
If, fair Thisbe—

QUINCE [*interrupting, horrified*]
O monstrous! O strange! We are haunted. Pray, masters! Fly, masters! Help!

[*QUINCE, SNUG, FLUTE, SNOUT, and STARVELING run screaming in all directions, leaving BOTTOM standing alone. PUCK whoops with delight and runs after them.*]

BOTTOM
Why do they run away?

[*Enter QUINCE, very cautiously, checking whether his eyes have fooled him; PUCK, unseen, creeps behind QUINCE.*]

QUINCE [*staring wide-eyed at the donkey head*]
Bless thee, Bottom! Thou art translated!

[*PUCK pinches QUINCE, who screams and exits running, with PUCK giggling fiendishly behind.*]

BOTTOM
I see their knavery! This is to make an ass of me, to frighten me. But I will not stir from this place. I will walk up and down here, and I will sing, and they shall hear I am not afraid.

translated: transformed

knavery: pranks, mischievous tricks

[*He sings, off-key, walking back and forth, at one point coming very near the sleeping TITANIA, who stirs, sits up, sees BOTTOM—and immediately falls in love. As he stops singing for a moment, perhaps to clear his throat or remember the next line of his song, TITANIA rises.*]

TITANIA [*her voice full of wonder and love*]
What angel wakes me from my flowery bed?

[*BOTTOM turns and sees her. He is not alarmed. TITANIA moves toward him.*]

I pray thee, gentle mortal, sing again!
Mine ear is much enamored of thy note.
So is mine eye enthrallèd to thy shape!
[*She wraps her arms around him.*]
O, I love thee!

BOTTOM [*calmly, reasonably*]
Methinks, mistress, you should have little reason
for that.

[*She begins stroking his muzzle, kissing his ears, etc.*]

And yet, to say the truth, reason and love keep little
company together nowadays.

TITANIA
Thou art as wise as thou art beautiful.

Act 3, Scene 1

enamored: filled with feelings of love

enthrallèd (pronounced as three syllables, en•thrall•ed): fascinated with, captured by

BOTTOM
Not so, neither.

[*Speaking matter-of-factly, he steps away from TITANIA.*]

But if I had wit enough to get out of this wood . . .

[*TITANIA extends her hand, which makes BOTTOM snap still, as though he has reached the end of an invisible rope.*]

TITANIA
Out of this wood do not desire to go!
Thou shalt remain here, whether thou wilt or no.

[*With one curling finger, she pulls him toward her.*]

I do love thee, and therefore, go with me.
I'll give thee fairies to attend on thee,
Peaseblossom! Cobweb! Moth! And Mustardseed!

[*The FAIRIES enter.*]

PEASEBLOSSOM
Ready!

COBWEB
And I!

wit: intelligence, mental sharpness

whether thou wilt or no: whether or not you want to

MOTH
And I!

MUSTARDSEED
And I!

TITANIA
Be kind and courteous to this gentleman.
Feed him with apricots and dewberries,
With purple grapes, green figs, and mulberries.
Bow to him, elves, and do him courtesies.

PEASEBLOSSOM [*bowing*]
Hail, mortal!

COBWEB [*bowing*]
Hail!

MOTH [*bowing*]
Hail!

MUSTARDSEED [*bowing*]
Hail!

TITANIA
Come, wait upon him. Lead him to my bower.

[*BOTTOM emits a loud "Hee-haw!"*]

Tie up my love's tongue. Bring him silently.

[*All exit.*]

Act 3, Scene 1

dewberries: sweet berries like blackberries

bower: a pleasant shady place; or, a lady's private room

SCENE 2: ANOTHER PART OF THE WOOD.

SPEAKER 1
That magic flower juice really works! The fairy queen is head-over-heels in love with Bottom.

SPEAKER 2 [*nudging SPEAKER 1 with elbow*]
Or maybe you should say "head-over-hooves."
[*giggles in appreciation of her or his own wit*]

SPEAKER 3 [*rescuing the play from SPEAKER 2's joke*]
Anyway, not far off, in another part of the wood, here comes Oberon, the fairy king.

[*Enter OBERON.*]

OBERON
I wonder if Titania be awaked,
And what it was that next came in her eye . . .

[*Enter PUCK, humming or whistling merrily.*]

How now, mad spirit?

PUCK [*excited and overjoyed*]
My mistress with a monster is in love!

[*PUCK dashes to OBERON's side; they mime the following conversation reported by the SPEAKERS.*]

SPEAKER 1
Puck tells Oberon how he came across the group of workmen rehearsing in the wood.

SPEAKER 2
And how he gave Bottom the head of a donkey.

SPEAKER 3
And how he left Bottom alone with the sleeping Fairy Queen, and chased all the other workmen away.

PUCK [*triumphantly concluding his account to OBERON*]
I led them on in this distracted fear
And left sweet Pyramus translated there,
When in that moment (so it came to pass)
Titania waked and straightway loved an ass!

OBERON
This falls out better than I could devise.
But hast thou yet latched the Athenian's eyes
With the love juice, as I did bid thee do?

PUCK
I took him sleeping—that is finished too.

[*HERMIA enters, followed closely by DEMETRIUS, panting. She looks around, desperately hoping to spot Lysander.*]

straightway (an old form of the word *straightaway*): at once, right away, immediately

falls out: happens

devise: plan

latched: caught

bid thee do: order you to do

OBERON
Stand close. This is the same Athenian.

PUCK [*"uh-oh" in his voice*]
This is the woman, but not this the man.

[*OBERON pulls PUCK aside and makes a gesture to render themselves invisible. They watch the scene.*]

DEMETRIUS
O, why rebuke you him that loves you so?

HERMIA
For thou, I fear, hast given me cause to curse
If thou hast slain Lysander in his sleep.
The sun was not so true unto the day
As he to me. Would he have stolen away
From sleeping Hermia?

DEMETRIUS
I am not guilty of Lysander's blood;
Nor is he dead, for aught that I can tell.

HERMIA [*pleading*]
I pray thee, tell me then that he is well.

DEMETRIUS
And if I could, what should I get therefore?*

[*He edges toward her, head forward, lips puckered for a kiss.*]

rebuke: express disapproval

slain: killed

for aught that I can tell: as far as I know

* In this line, "therefore" is pronounced with the accent on the second syllable: there*fore*.

HERMIA [*angrily*]
A privilege never to see me more!

[*She stomps on his foot and exits.*]

DEMETRIUS
There is no following her in this fierce vein.
Here therefore for a while I will remain.

[*He yawns, lies down, and sleeps.*]

OBERON [*in amazed disbelief to PUCK*]
What hast thou done?!

[*PUCK grins sheepishly. He and OBERON mime the following conversation related by the SPEAKERS:*]

SPEAKER 1
Oberon wants Puck to fix his mistake. He tells Puck to go find Helena and bring her back here.

SPEAKER 2
In the meantime, Oberon will use the magic flower to charm Demetrius . . .

SPEAKER 3
So that when Demetrius wakes, he will see Helena and fall in love with her.

Act 3, Scene 2

OBERON [*impatiently, to PUCK*]
About the wood go swifter than the wind!

PUCK
I go, I go. Look how I go!

[*PUCK exits in haste. OBERON squeezes the magic flower juice in DEMETRIUS's eyes, saying:*]

OBERON
Flower of this purple dye,
When his love he doth espy,
Let her shine as gloriously
As the Venus of the sky.

[*Enter PUCK.*]

PUCK
Captain of our fairy band,
Helena is here at hand,
And the youth, mistook by me.
Shall we their fond pageant see?
Lord, what fools these mortals be!

OBERON
Stand aside. The noise they make
Will cause Demetrius to awake.

[*OBERON and PUCK step aside, invisible, as HELENA enters, followed by LYSANDER. They do not see the sleeping DEMETRIUS.*]

espy: catch sight of

Venus of the sky: the planet Venus, which can often be seen shining brightly just after sunset or in the hours before sunrise

fond pageant: foolish display

mortals: human beings

LYSANDER [*pleading*]
Why should you think that I should woo in scorn?
Look, when I vow, I weep.

[*He sniffs and wipes an eye.*]

HELENA
These vows are Hermia's!

LYSANDER
Demetrius loves her, and he loves not you.

[*HELENA turns away and bumps into DEMETRIUS, who wakes and sees her.*]

DEMETRIUS [*rising*]
O Helena, goddess, nymph, perfect, divine!

[*HELENA looks back and forth between the two men who have been magically charmed to love her. Her expression turns from confused (What's going on?) to angry (Oh, I see what you're up to).*]

HELENA
O spite! O spite! I see you all are bent
To set against me for your merriment.
You both are rivals, and love Hermia,
And now both rivals, to mock Helena!

that I should woo in scorn: that in trying to win your love I am playing a mean trick

vow: promise (that he loves her)

spite: mean and hurtful intentions

bent: determined

rivals: competitors

LYSANDER [*shoving DEMETRIUS's shoulder*]
You are unkind, Demetrius. Be not so,
For you love Hermia. This you know I know.

DEMETRIUS [*shoving back*]
Lysander, keep thy Hermia. I will none.
If e'er I loved her, all that love is gone.

[*Enter HERMIA, panting. She sees LYSANDER.*]

HERMIA
Lysander—found!
[*She rushes to him.*]
But why unkindly didst thou leave me so?

[*LYSANDER backs away from her.*]

LYSANDER [*"yuck" in his voice*]
Why seek'st thou me?
The hate I bear thee made me leave thee.

HERMIA
Hate me! It cannot be!
Am not I Hermia? Are not you Lysander?

LYSANDER
Ay, by my life—
And never do desire to see thee more.

I will none: I have no desire for her

Why seek'st thou me?: Why are you looking for me?

by my life: an expression of strong feeling, meaning "absolutely, certainly"

HERMIA
You speak not as you think. It cannot be!

[HELENA points at HERMIA and cries out accusingly:]

HELENA
Lo, she is one of this confederacy!
Injurious Hermia! Most ungrateful maid!
Have you joined with them in scorning your
　poor friend?

HERMIA
I am amazed at your passionate words!
I scorn you not. It seems that you scorn me.

HELENA
Have you not set Lysander, as a jest,
To follow me and praise my eyes and face?
And made your other love, Demetrius,
To call me goddess, nymph, divine, and rare?

HERMIA
I understand not what you mean by this!

[LYSANDER runs to HELENA'S side and takes her hand.]

LYSANDER
Helena, I love thee! By my life, I do!

[DEMETRIUS runs to her other side and takes her hand.]

confederacy: a group joined for a common purpose

jest: joke

DEMETRIUS
I say I love thee more than he can do!

HERMIA [*In despair*]
O me!
[*suddenly furious, turning to HELENA*]
You trickster, you cankerblossom!
You thief of love! What, have you come by night
And stolen my love's heart from him?

HELENA [*to DEMETRIUS and LYSANDER*]
I pray you, though you mock me, gentlemen,
Let her not hurt me. You perhaps may think,
Because she is something lower than myself,
That I can match her.

HERMIA
How low am I, thou painted maypole? Speak!
How low am I? I am not yet so low
But that my nails can reach unto thine eyes!

[*She leaps at HELENA, but the men stop her.*]

HELENA
O, though she be but little, she is fierce.

HERMIA
"Little" again! Nothing but "low" and "little"!
Let me come at her!

cankerblossom: a worm that destroys flowers

lower: shorter

can match her: can equal her in a fight

maypole: a tall pole, often decorated with flowers, around which people dance while holding ribbons attached to the pole

thine: your

[*As LYSANDER pulls HELENA aside protectively, he says to HERMIA:*]

LYSANDER
Get you gone, you bead, you acorn!

[*As DEMETRIUS pulls HELENA away from LYSANDER, he says to him:*]

DEMETRIUS
Speak not for Helena; take not her part!

LYSANDER [*pumping his fists at DEMETRIUS*]
Now follow, if thou darest, to fight for Helena.

DEMETRIUS
Follow! Nay, I'll go with thee!

[*LYSANDER and DEMETRIUS exit, pumping their fists at each other. HERMIA approaches HELENA threateningly.*]

HERMIA
You, mistress—

[*As HELENA retreats from HERMIA, she says:*]

HELENA
Your hands than mine are quicker for a fray,
My legs are longer though, to run away!

[*Exit, running from HERMIA.*]

take not her part: do not take her side

if thou darest: if you dare

fray: fight

HERMIA
I am amazed, and know not what to say!

[*Exit, running after HELENA. PUCK and OBERON step forward.*]

OBERON [*sternly to PUCK*]
This is thy negligence.

PUCK
Believe me, king of shadows, I mistook.

OBERON
Thou see'st these lovers seek a place to fight.
Hie therefore, Robin, overcast the night . . .

[*They mime the following conversation related by the SPEAKERS:*]

SPEAKER 1
Oberon orders Puck to clean up the mess he has made. He tells Puck to cast a deep fog over the wood . . .

[*PUCK casts his spell, perhaps spinning with arms raised high.*]

SPEAKER 2
So that the four young lovers will not see each other . . .

Act 3, Scene 2   143

negligence: carelessness

hie: go quickly

[*DEMETRIUS, LYSANDER, HELENA, AND HERMIA enter from different directions, squinting, hands held in front of them, passing near but not seeing each other.*]

SPEAKER 3
And so they won't beat the stuffing out of each other!

SPEAKER 1
Puck then leads the lovers back to this same spot.

[*PUCK magically guides them; they do not see each other.*]

PUCK
Up and down, up and down,
I will lead them up and down.
I am feared in field and town.
Goblin, lead them up and down.

SPEAKER 2
Exhausted, they collapse into sleep.

[*They fall asleep.*]

SPEAKER 3
And now Puck, with a second flower, can undo the charm on Lysander's eyes.

[*PUCK receives the second flower from OBERON.*]

Act 3, Scene 2

OBERON
When they next wake, all this derision
Shall seem a dream and fruitless vision.

[*He exits.*]

PUCK [*to the sleeping LYSANDER*]
I'll apply
To your eye,
Gentle lover, remedy.

[*PUCK squeezes the flower juice on the LYSANDER's eyes. Then PUCK rises and addresses the audience:*]

Jack shall have Jill,
Naught shall go ill,
And all shall be well!

[*He exits, laughing.*]

Act 3, Scene 2

derision: scornful mockery
fruitless: empty

naught shall go ill: nothing will go wrong

ACT 4

SCENE 1: THE SAME PLACE IN THE WOOD, WITH THE FOUR YOUNG LOVERS ASLEEP, WHERE THEY REMAIN UNOBSERVED.

[Enter TITANIA, BOTTOM (with donkey head), and FAIRIES; OBERON, unseen, follows closely behind, watching all that goes on.]

TITANIA [*to BOTTOM*]
Come, sit thee down upon this flowery bed,
While I kiss thy fair large ears, my gentle joy.

BOTTOM
Where's Peaseblossom?

PEASEBLOSSOM
Ready!

BOTTOM
Scratch my head, Master Peaseblossom.

[PEASEBLOSSOM and the other FAIRIES gently scratch BOTTOM's head.]

BOTTOM
I must to the barber's, for methinks I am marvelous hairy about the face. And I am such a tender ass, if my hair do but tickle me, I must scratch.

Act 4, Scene 1

TITANIA
O say, sweet love, what thou <u>desirest</u> to eat.

BOTTOM
Truly, I could munch your good dry oats. Or a handful or two of dried peas.
[*He yawns.*]
But, I pray you, let none of your people stir me. I have an exposition of sleep* come upon me.

TITANIA
Sleep thou, and I will wind thee in my arms.
Fairies, begone!

[*The FAIRIES tiptoe off.*]

O, how I love thee! How I dote on thee!

[*As TITANIA and BOTTOM sleep, OBERON advances and PUCK enters.*]

OBERON [*to PUCK*]
See'st thou this sweet sight?
Her dotage** now I do begin to pity.
And now I have the boy, I will undo
This hateful imperfection of her eyes.

[*He kneels and squeezes the juice of the second flower in TITANIA's eyes.*]

desirest: desire, want

* Bottom mistakenly refers to "an exposition of sleep." He means "a disposition to sleep" (a feeling that he wants to sleep).

** In referring to "her dotage," Oberon means Titania's doting upon, or extreme affection for, Bottom.

Be as thou wast wont to be;
See as thou wast wont to see.
Now, my Titania, wake you, my sweet queen.

TITANIA
My Oberon! What visions have I seen!
Methought I was enamored of an ass.

OBERON [*pointing to BOTTOM*]
There lies your love.

TITANIA [*shocked*]
How came these things to pass?

OBERON
My gentle Puck, take this transformèd scalp
From off the head of this Athenian swain;
That, he awaking when the others do,
May all to Athens back again repair
And think no more of this night's accidents
But as the fierce vexation of a dream.

[*As PUCK restores BOTTOM to his normal form, he says:*]

PUCK
Now, when thou wakest, with thine own fool's eyes peep.

OBERON
Come, my queen, take hands with me.
We will tomorrow midnight solemnly
Dance in Duke Theseus's house triumphantly.

Act 4, Scene 1

be as thou wast wont to be: be as you usually are

methought: I thought

enamored of: in love with

transformèd: (pronounced as three syllables, trans·form·ed): completely changed in appearance or shape

scalp: surface of the head

swain: a country youth

repair: go

fierce vexation: strong disturbance or confusion

solemnly: seriously, formally

triumphantly: with rejoicing and celebration

There shall the pairs of faithful lovers be
Wedded, with Theseus, all in jollity.

PUCK
Fairy king, attend, and mark—
I do hear the morning lark.

TITANIA
Come, my lord, and in our flight
Tell me how it came this night
That I sleeping here was found
With these mortals on the ground.

[*All exit. As they leave, enter THESEUS and HIPPOLYTA, dressed for hunting (perhaps with bows and arrows), followed by EGEUS. At first they do not see the sleeping lovers or BOTTOM.*]

THESEUS [*romantically, to HIPPOLYTA*]
My love shall hear the music of my hounds.
We will, fair queen, up to the mountain's top,
And . . .

EGEUS [*interrupting, alarmed*]
My lord, this is my daughter here asleep!
And this, Lysander! This Demetrius is!
This, Helena!

[*Hearing EGEUS, the lovers stir slowly awake, groggy and confused.*]

jollity: lively celebration

mark: notice, pay attention to

the music of my hounds: the barking of my hunting dogs

THESEUS [*amused*]
Good morrow, friends. Saint Valentine is past.
I pray you all, stand up.

[*They stand, HERMIA by LYSANDER, and HELENA by DEMETRIUS. THESEUS addresses LYSANDER and DEMETRIUS.*]

I know you two are rival enemies.
How comes this gentle concord in the world?

LYSANDER
My lord, I shall reply amazedly,
Half sleep, half waking—but as yet, I swear,
I cannot truly say how I came here.
But, as I think—for truly would I speak—
I came with Hermia hither. Our intent
Was to be gone from Athens, where we might,
Without the peril of the Athenian law . . .

[*EGEUS, who has been simmering with anger, now boils over.*]

EGEUS
Enough, enough, my lord! You have enough!
I beg the law, the law upon his head!
They would have stolen away; they would!

THESEUS
Egeus, I will overbear your will.
For in the temple by and by with us

Saint Valentine is past: Valentine's Day is already past.

concord: harmony, peace

peril: danger

overbear your will: overrule your wish

These couples shall <u>eternally be knit</u>.
Away with us to Athens! Come, Hippolyta.

[*Exit THESEUS, HIPPOLYTA, and EGEUS.*]

DEMETRIUS
Are you sure
That we are awake? It seems to me
That yet we sleep, we dream. Do not you think
The duke was here, and <u>bid us</u> follow him?

HERMIA
<u>Yea</u>, and my father.

HELENA
And Hippolyta.

LYSANDER
And he did bid us follow.

DEMETRIUS
Why, then, we are awake! Let's follow him
And by the way let us <u>recount</u> our dreams.

[*They exit together, laughing and talking.*]

SPEAKER 1
Well, it looks like everything worked out well after all!

SPEAKER 2
I love a happy ending!

eternally be knit: forever be joined together (in marriage)

bid us: commanded us, invited us

yea (pronounced "yay"): yes

recount (accent on second syllable, re*count*): tell about

SPEAKER 3
Um, guys, it's not quite the ending.
[*SPEAKER 3 points at BOTTOM, who suddenly wakes with a start.*]

BOTTOM
When my cue comes, call me, and I will answer!
[*He rises, dusts himself off, and looks around. Realizing he is alone, he calls out loudly:*]
Peter Quince! Flute, the bellows-mender! Snout, the tinker! Starveling! God's my life, stolen hence, and left me asleep!
[*A sudden thought alarms him. He feels his face—then, relieved to find it normal . . .*]
I have had a most rare vision. I have had a dream past the wit of man to say what dream it was. Man is but an ass if he go about to expound this dream.*
Methought I was . . .
[*He checks his ears.*]
And methought I had . . .
[*He looks to see if he has a tail. Then, inspired:*]
I will get Peter Quince to write a ballad of this dream! It shall be called Bottom's Dream—because it hath no bottom.** And I will sing it at the end of our play before the duke!

[*He exits.*]

stolen hence: sneaked away

* Bottom is saying that a man would be a fool to attempt to explain his dream.

ballad: a poem or song that tells a story

** In saying that his dream "hath no bottom," Bottom suggests that it was mysterious and beyond understanding.

ACT 5

SCENE 1: ATHENS. THE PALACE OF DUKE THESEUS.

SPEAKER 1
And so we are back in Athens, at the palace of Duke Theseus...

SPEAKER 2
Where, earlier today, three couples have been happily joined in marriage.

[*As music plays, enter, arm in arm, THESEUS and HIPPOLYTA, DEMETRIUS and HELENA, LYSANDER and HERMIA. They take a turn around the stage and then take their seats.*]

SPEAKER 3 [*as music fades*]
And now the evening has come, and it is time for the festivities to celebrate the weddings.

THESEUS
Come now—what songs, what dances shall we have?
What <u>revels</u> are at hand? How shall we <u>beguile</u>
The lazy time, if not with some delight?

[*Enter PHILOSTRATE, snobbish and picky, who has organized the evening's entertainments, and who has had a very long day of it.*]

revels: lively entertainments

beguile: pleasantly pass (the time)

PHILOSTRATE
A play there is, my lord, some ten words long—
Which is as brief as I have known a play—
But by ten words, my lord, it is too long.

THESEUS
What are they that do play it?

PHILOSTRATE
Hard-handed men that work in Athens here,
Which never labored in their minds till now.

THESEUS [*amused and interested*]
And we will hear it.

PHILOSTRATE
No, my noble lord! It is not for you!

THESEUS
I will hear that play.
Go, bring them in.

[*Exit PHILOSTRATE, heaving a deep sigh.*]

HIPPOLYTA [*glancing at the young couples*]
'Tis strange, my Theseus, that these lovers spoke of.

THESEUS
More strange than true.
Lovers and madmen have such seething brains!

hard-handed men: men whose hands have been toughened by hard work

seething brains: boiling imaginations

HIPPOLYTA
Joy and fresh days of love accompany their hearts!

[*Enter PHILOSTRATE, leading the workmen, in their costumes. PHILOSTRATE pulls a reluctant PETER QUINCE, shaking with stage fright, to center stage.*]

PHILOSTRATE
So please your grace, the Prologue.

[*Exit PHILOSTRATE. QUINCE bows awkwardly. As he speaks, his voice is shaky at first, then slowly gains confidence.*]

QUINCE
Gentles, perchance you wonder at this show.
But wonder on, till truth make all things plain.
This man is Pyramus, if you would know.

[*BOTTOM steps forth with a showy bow.*]

This beauteous lady Thisbe is, certain.

[*FLUTE, embarrassed, steps forward and curtsies.*]

This man, with lime and rough-cast, doth present
Wall, that vile Wall which did these lovers sunder.

[*SNOUT, costumed as Wall, awkwardly tries to bow.*]

Act 5, Scene 1

the Prologue: the actor who introduces the play

lime: a white chalky substance
rough-cast: plaster used on outside walls
sunder: split apart

This man, with lantern, dog, and bush of thorn,*
Presenteth Moonshine.

[*STARVELING steps forth, eagerly displaying his props.*]

This grisly beast, or Lion known by name,
The trusty Thisbe, coming first by night,
Did scare away, or rather did affright.

[*SNUG steps forth and waves a timid paw.*]

Let Lion, Moonshine, Wall, and lovers twain
At large discourse, while here they do remain.

[*The nobles politely applaud. QUINCE bows and exits, followed by FLUTE-Thisbe and STARVELING-Moonshine. BOTTOM-Pyramus moves to one side as SNOUT-Wall takes center stage.*]

SNOUT [*as Wall*]
In this same interlude it doth befall
That I, one Snout by name, present a wall.
And such a wall, as I would have you think,
That had in it a crannied hole or chink,
Through which the lovers, Pyramus and Thisbe,
Did whisper often very secretly.

[*He extends one hand, making a wide space between the middle finger and ring finger.*]

> * The "bush of thorn" may refer to old folktales that depict the "man in the moon" carrying a bundle of sticks on his back.

grisly: gruesome, frightful

affright: frighten

twain: two

at large discourse: speak at length

befall: happen

crannied: having small cracks or openings

chink: a crack or narrow opening

THESEUS
Would you desire lime and rock to speak better?

DEMETRIUS
It is the wittiest partition that ever I heard discourse, my lord.

[Enter BOTTOM as Pyramus.]

THESEUS *[amused]*
Pyramus draws near the wall—silence!

BOTTOM *[as Pyramus, in a booming voice, tragically romantic, with many excessive gestures]*
O grim-look'd night! O night with hue so black!
O night, which ever art when day is not!
O night, O night! Alack, alack, alack!
I fear my Thisbe's promise is forgot!
And thou, O wall, O sweet, O lovely wall,
That stand'st between her father's ground and mine!
Thou wall, O wall, O sweet and lovely wall,
Show me thy chink, to blink through with mine eye!

[Wall holds up his hand with space between his fingers. Pyramus looks through the "chink."]

Thanks, courteous wall.
But what see I? No Thisbe do I see.
O wicked wall, through whom I see no bliss!
Cursed be thy stones for thus deceiving me!

partition: something that divides (such as a wall)

hue: a color or shade

[*BOTTOM whacks Wall—and from SNOUT's reaction, we can see this was not planned.*]

THESEUS [*making a witty comment to HIPPOLYTA*]
The wall, methinks, should curse at him.

[*BOTTOM—speaking as himself, not as Pyramus—addresses THESEUS.*]

BOTTOM
No, in truth, sir, he should not. "Deceiving me" is Thisbe's cue. She is to enter now, and I am to spy her through the wall. You shall see. Yonder she comes!

[*Enter FLUTE as Thisbe.*]

FLUTE [*as Thisbe, in a high voice*]
O wall, full often hast thou heard my moans,
For parting my fair Pyramus and me!

BOTTOM [*as Pyramus*]
I see a voice! Now will I to the chink,
To spy if I can hear my Thisbe's face.

[*He calls through Wall's parted fingers.*]

Thisbe!

FLUTE [*as Thisbe*]
My love! Thou art my love, I think.

BOTTOM [*as Pyramus*]
O kiss me through the hole of this vile wall!

[*Pyramus and Thisbe make loud, long kissing noises on each side of Wall's fingers. Wall is not pleased.*]

FLUTE [*as Thisbe*]
I kiss the wall's hole, not your lips at all.

BOTTOM [*as Pyramus*]
Wilt thou at Ninny's tomb meet me straightway?

[*QUINCE groans.*]

FLUTE [*as Thisbe*]
Come life or death, I come without delay.

[*Pyramus and Thisbe exit in opposite directions, blowing kisses. Wall bows as best he can and then exits, saying:*]

SNOUT [*as Wall*]
Thus have I, Wall, my part dischargèd so;
And, being done, thus Wall away doth go.

HIPPOLYTA
This is the silliest stuff that ever I heard!

[*Enter Lion and Moonshine.*]

Act 5, Scene 1

dischargèd (pronounced as three syllables, dis•charg•ed): completed

THESEUS
Here come two noble beasts in, a man and a lion.

SNUG [*as Lion*]
You, ladies, you whose gentle hearts do fear
The smallest monstrous mouse that creeps on floor,
May now perchance both quake and tremble here,
When lion rough in wildest rage doth roar.

[*He roars—meekly—and then quickly reassures the ladies:*]

Then know that I, one Snug the joiner am,
Nor else no lion.

[*SNUG steps aside.*]

THESEUS
A very gentle beast, of a good conscience.

[*STARVELING steps forward with a bundle of sticks, a lantern, and a stuffed toy dog.*]

STARVELING [*as Moonshine*]
This lantern doth the shining moon present;
Myself the man in the moon do seem to be.

[*He opens his mouth—no words come out. He struggles to remember. Frustrated, he whacks his head with the stuffed dog, and then he says:*]

perchance: perhaps

nor else no lion: not a lion at all

All that I have to say, is, to tell you that the lantern is the moon; I, the man in the moon; this thorn-bush, my thorn-bush; and this dog, my dog!

HIPPOLYTA
I am a-weary of this moon—would he would change!

[*Moonshine looks very sad.*]

[*Enter Thisbe.*]

FLUTE [*as Thisbe*]
This is old Ninny's tomb. [*looking around.*] Where is my love?

[*Enter SNUG as Lion, advancing toward Thisbe.*]

SNUG [*as Lion*]
Roarrr!

[*Thisbe runs off with a shriek, dropping her shawl, which Lion picks up and chews fiercely.*]

HERMIA
Well roared, Lion!

HELENA
Well run, Thisbe!

Act 5, Scene 1   179

would: I wish that

HIPPOLYTA
Well shone, Moon. Truly, the moon shines with a good grace.

[*Moonshine smiles broadly.*]

[*Lion shakes Thisbe's shawl, lets it drop, and exits.*]

LYSANDER
And so the lion vanished.

[*Enter Pyramus.*]

DEMETRIUS
And then came Pyramus.

BOTTOM [*as Pyramus*]
Sweet Moon, I thank thee for thy sunny beams.
I thank thee, Moon, for shining now so bright;
For, by thy gracious, golden, glittering gleams,
I trust to take of truest Thisbe sight.

[*He sees Thisbe's shawl.*]

But stay, O spite!
But mark, poor knight.

[*He picks up the shawl—despair!*]

stay: stop

spite: something hurtful, upsetting, distressing

Eyes, do you see?
How can it be?
O dainty duck! O dear!

Thy mantle good—
What, stained with blood!
Out, sword, and wound
The pap of Pyramus.

[*He stabs himself in the armpit with a toy sword.*]

Thus die I, thus, thus, thus.
[*He stabs himself again and again with each "thus."*]

Now am I dead,
Now am I fled,
My soul is in the sky!
Tongue, lose thy light.
Moon take thy flight—

[*Exit Moonshine, waving "bye-bye."*]

Now die, die, die, die, die.

[*With each "die" he dies in five different and increasingly ridiculous ways. When he is finally finished:*]

THESEUS
With the help of a surgeon he might yet recover.

[*Enter Thisbe*]

mantle: shawl

pap: breast

FLUTE [*as Thisbe*]
Asleep, my love?

[*She kneels down and shakes Pyramus—and reacts with horror!*]

What, dead, my dove?
O Pyramus, arise!
Speak, speak!
Dead? Dead!

These lily lips,
This cherry nose,
These yellow cowslip cheeks,
Are gone, are gone!

Come, trusty sword.

[*She takes the toy sword.*]

Come, blade!

[*She stabs herself in the armpit.*]

And farewell, friends.
Thus Thisbe ends.

[*She falls on Pyramus, who grunts audibly.*]

Adieu, adieu, adieu.

Act 5, Scene 1

cowslip: a yellow flower

adieu (French word, pronounced uh•dyoo): farewell

[*She dies. The nobles applaud. FLUTE and BOTTOM jump up, the other workmen rush in, and all bow randomly.*]

BOTTOM [*as the applause ends*]
Will it please you to see the epilogue?

THESEUS [*responding immediately, alarmed*]
No epilogue, I pray you! [*then, reassuringly*] For your play needs no excuse.

[*The nobles applaud again, briefly. The workmen take one last bow and exit, patting each other on the back, shaking hands, high-fiving.*]

Lovers, to bed; 'tis almost fairy time.
I fear we shall out-sleep the coming morn.
Sweet friends, to bed.

[*The couples exit, hand in hand. As they leave, PUCK sneaks in, unseen by them, carrying a broom.*]

PUCK [*directly addressing the audience*]
I am sent with broom before,
To sweep the dust behind the door.

[*PUCK sweeps for a few seconds and then takes center stage. As PUCK speaks the following epilogue, all the actors, including the SPEAKERS, enter and line up.*]

Act 5, Scene 1

epilogue: a speech at the end of a play that comments on what happened in the play

morn: morning

If we shadows have offended,
Think but this, and all is mended:
That you have but slumbered here
While these visions did appear.
And this weak and idle theme,
No more yielding but a dream.

Gentles, do not reprehend.
If you pardon, we will mend.
So, good night unto you all.
Give me your hands,* if we be friends,
And Robin shall restore amends.

[*All bow as one.*]

mended: repaired, fixed, made right

idle: silly

no more yielding but a dream: producing no more than if the audience had been dreaming

gentles: ladies and gentlemen

reprehend: speak harshly and critically

pardon: forgive our faults

mend: improve

restore amends: make up for any faults

* In saying, "Give me your hands," Puck is asking the audience to clap in applause.

Cover and Title Page Illustration by
PAINTING / Alamy Stock Photo

Text Illustrations by
Album / Alamy Stock Photo / 29
Artokoloro Quint Lox Limited / Alamy Stock Photo / IX
BLM Collection / Alamy Stock Photo / 24
Charles Walker Collection / Alamy Stock Photo / 1
FALKENSTEINFOTO / Alamy Stock Photo / X
Historic Images / Alamy Stock Photo / 16
Ivan Pesic / 30
Lebrecht Music & Arts / Alamy Stock Photo / 10
World History Archive / Alamy Stock Photo / VI

Story adapted from
"A Midsummer Night's Dream" in Progressive Road to
Reading: Fifth Reader (California State Series), ed.
Georgine Burchill, William Ettinger, and Edgar Dubs
Shimer (Sacramento: Silver, Burdett, and Co., 1917). / 1-27